JiGGLE
WiGGLE
PRANCE
by Sally Noll

FOR TORY

The full-color art work, gouache paintings, was mechanically color-separated and reproduced in four colors.
The text typeface is Avant Garde Bold.

Publisher, Greenwillow Books, a division of William Morrow & Company, Inc., 105 Madison Avenue, New York, N.Y. 10016.
Printed in Hong Kong by South China Printing Co.
First Edition

10 9 8 7 6 5 4 3 2 1

Library of Congress
Cataloging-in-Publication Data

Noll, Sally.

Jiggle wiggle prance.

Summary: Includes Illustrations of animals acting out such rhyming action words as "pull, flop, hop" and "dance, prance."

1. English language—Rhyme —Juvenile literature.
2. Vocabulary—Juvenile literature.
[1. English language—Rhyme.
2. Vocabulary]   I. Title.
PE1517.N6 1987   428.1   86-18322
ISBN 0-688-06760-3
ISBN 0-688-06761-1 (lib. bdg.)

WALK

ROCK DROP

PUSH

PULL   FLOP

HOP   **SPIN**

DANCE

JIGGLE WIGGLE

PRANCE

FOLLOW   FLY

SWING

HOBBLE

WOBBLE   FLING

JUMP

RUN   RACE

SKIP   TRIP

PACE

RIDE **DRIVE**

ROLL

SKATE　　　　**STRIDE**

STROLL

CLIMB

SLIDE   **FALL**

AND THAT'S ALL.